THE FUNNIEST HALLOWEEN JOKE IN ST. LOUIS

Written and illustrated by Ryan Nusbickel

THE FUNNIEST HALLOWEEN JOKE IN ST. LOUIS

Copyright © 2018
Ryan Nusbickel
Nusbickel Books LLC
All rights reserved

ISBN-978-1720604419

NUSBICKEL
books

For Kasey, Parker, and home-made costumes from the 80's.

SPOILER ALERT:
Only St. Louis kids tell Halloween jokes.

It's true. Ask any St. Louis transplant - they never told jokes to earn candy on Halloween when they were growing up elsewhere. And they'll tell you this local tradition left them slightly baffled on their first Halloween in St. Louis. On the contrary, ask any original St. Louis native who later moved away. They'll confirm that not one Halloween joke is told outside the St. Louis area.* But there were plenty of awkward Halloween moments when they demanded jokes from bewildered trick-or-treaters. The kids my wife badgered when she was in college in Ohio may be permanently scarred. But here in St. Louis, this charming transaction for Halloween candy goes back generations. While its origin remains a mystery, most agree that it is rooted in the idea of "dancing for one's dinner."

How could I possibly do a St. Louis Halloween book without making our delicious custom the centerpiece? Yes, we tell jokes, and you should too. It's hilarious.

-Ryan Nusbickel

* Trick-or-treaters in Des Moines, Iowa tell jokes on October 30th, known locally as Beggars' Night, but they do not tell jokes on Halloween.

The world's hardest-working trick-or-treaters live in the Lou.
The only place on the planet that tells Halloween jokes - it's true!

5.

It's a mystery why St. Louis began this funny Halloween feat.

Did it start with a couple of Cubs jokes designed to get an extra treat?

Whatever the reason, this Halloween season Joe is going for the gold.
He vows to write the funniest Halloween joke ever told.

You see, Joe loved chocolate, lollipops, and all those other treats.

And he knew the funnier his joke, the more candy he could eat!

10.

So, Joe toiled over his gag, working both day and night.
Every word had to be hilarious. The timing had to be just right!
11.

Finally he had it!   The funniest Halloween joke ever written.

He tested it on his dog who nearly needed medical attention.

He whispered it to his parents who laughed themselves on the floor.

14.

He shared it with a family of cardinals nesting above his door.

He told it to a group of Chicago sports fans entering a corn maze.

16.

The corn wiggled with every giggle, and they were lost for days.

And on Halloween night, some West County witches laughed until they groaned,

And these South City skeletons nearly broke their funny bones.

His zinger made these Soulard specters throw Mardi Gras beads and laugh.

20.

His joke caused some Maryland Heights mummies to become nearly unwrapped.

21.

He told his joke to some Elsah eagles who nearly had a meltdown.

And he shared it with some werewolves who just arrived from Dogtown.

But before Joe could start trick-or-treating, a gust of wind blew by,

And it grabbed Joe's joke. His gag wasn't just the funniest. It could fly.

"Grab that joke!" Joe called to a boy dressed as a bluesman with a trombone.

He wasn't able to catch the joke in time, so he told Joe one of his own.

Joe waived down some other trick-or-treaters dressed like a barbecue.

28.

But their hands came up empty, so they shared their jokes with Joe too.

The joke flew by two trick-or-treaters dressed up as the Show-Me State.

Missouree and Missourah missed it, so a joke they did donate.

And finally, just as Joe nearly had the joke in his grasp
It took off in the Halloween sky on a final windy gasp.

32.

He once had the funniest gag ever, but now Joe was flat broke.

That's when he heard a voice say, "Happy Halloween. What's your joke?"

34.

Joe froze. Then, he remembered he did have jokes to recite.
The jokes told to him by the trick-or-treaters who tried to help him that night.

Joe rattled off all the jokes and was rewarded with candy galore.

He didn't need the funniest joke to land this Halloween score.

No one knows where the funniest Halloween joke finally landed.

Maybe we should check with those Chicago fans in the maze. Still stranded...

So remember, trick-or-treaters up in Seattle often will get wet.

Florida trick-or-treaters go in shorts, because it's not cold there yet.

Trick-or-treaters down in Texas wear their boots - it's true.

But the hardest working trick-or-treaters live in the Lou.

Here's hoping *your* Halloween is terrific through and through!

DON'T GET CAUGHT WITHOUT YOUR HALLOWEEN JOKE!

1) What does a cardinal say on Halloween?

"Trick or tweet!"

2) How do you know if a bakery is haunted?

They only serve "boo-ey butter cake."

3) Why are vampires awesome baseball players?

They've got great bats.

4. How do you know a ghost is a Chicago sports fan?

All he does is boo.

5. Why don't zombies ever win at trivia nights?

Because they answer every question with:
"AUUGGGGGHHHHH!!!"

6. Why do mummies hate going out for slingers?

Everyone wants to use them as a napkin.

7. How do you know Dracula is a hoosier?

He still has his Christmas lights up on
his coffin.

About the Author and Illustrator

Winners of the Honey Comb Kindergarten Halloween costume contest were announced at the Great Pumpkin pinata party held at the school this week. They are (l-r front) Jill Per- menter, Ryan Nusbickel and Jason Salmon (back row) Angela Martindale, Lisa Odom and Matt Boes. Staff photo.

The author/illustrator, pictured above as "Ryan Robot." His mother, Gloria Nusbickel, made his sophisticated costume with a garbage bag and milk jug mask.
Source: The Times-Picayune, 1979

As a decorated costume contest-winner, **Ryan Nusbickel** has always loved Halloween. An Emmy-winning, former TV reporter, Ryan has written and illustrated several children's books including *My Pet Arch, The St. Louis Night Before Christmas, Cloudy with a Chance of Toasted Rav, The St. Louis 12 Days of Christmas,* and *"Who Moved My Gooey Butter Cake?!."* All of Ryan's books can be purchased via www.nusbickelbooks.com.

Ryan lives in St. Louis with his wife and two daughters, who are both world-class Halloween joke-tellers.

Make your high school proud. Collect all of Ryan's books.

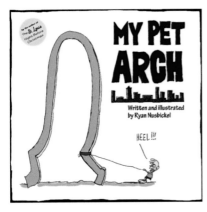

"The book for the St. Louisan who has everything."

-FEAST MAGAZINE

Ryan's books can be purchased at over fifty area retailers and on his website : www.nusbickelbooks.com.

Made in the USA
Lexington, KY
26 October 2018